STEP INTO THE WORLD OF

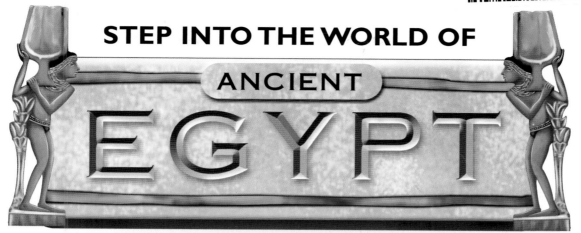

ANCIENT

EGYPT

CONTENTS

CONTENTS

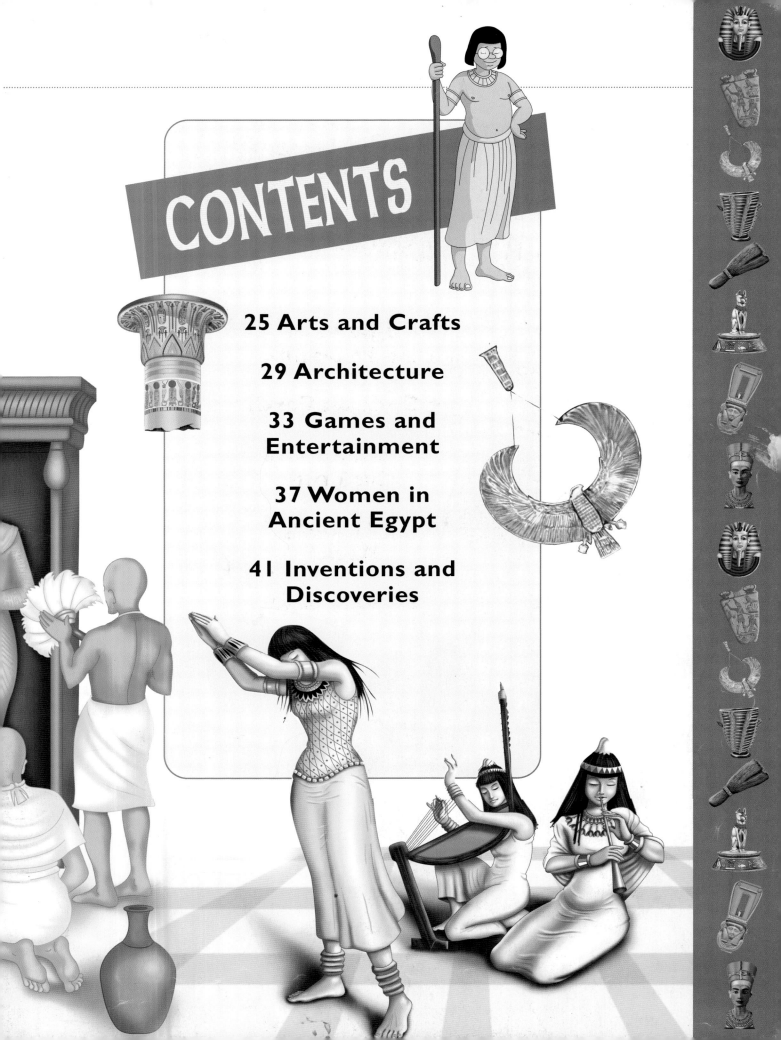

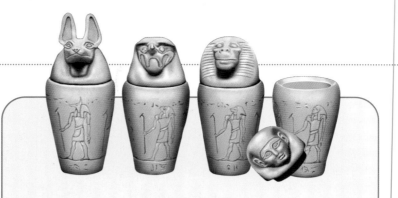

This is a Grandreams Book
This edition published in 2004

Grandreams Books Ltd
4 North Parade, Bath BA1 1LF, UK

Designed and packaged by
Q2A Design Studio

Printed in China

LAND OF THE PHARAOHS

Ancient Egypt is one of the world's longest-lasting civilisations. Its rulers (pharaohs) turned it into one of the most powerful empires ever.

Remarkable Rulers

Queen Hatshepsut was the first female pharaoh of Egypt, while Cleopatra VII was the last. Another legendary ruler was Ramses II, under whose reign the Egyptian empire reached its peak. Perhaps the most famed pharaoh of all time was Tutankhamun. At the age of nine, he became the youngest pharaoh and was also known as the 'boy king'. Although Tutankhamun was not the most important of rulers, he became famous when his tomb was uncovered as the only unrobbed Egyptian royal tomb ever!

Pharaoh Power

Pharaohs were believed to have been sent to earth by the gods in heaven. They were worshipped like gods and were seen as the spiritual link between the gods and the common people.

Pharaohs lived in palaces and possessed enormous wealth. During their travels, they would sit in carrying chairs. Cushioned seats were attached to poles so that the chair could be lifted on men's shoulders.

Pharaohs and other important people travelled from one place to another on luxurious carrying chairs

LAND OF THE PHARAOHS

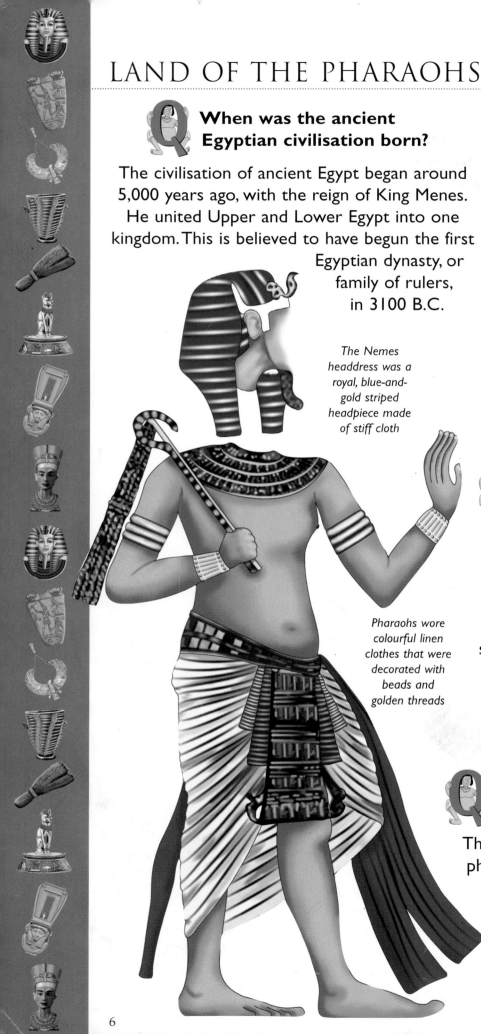

 Q When was the ancient Egyptian civilisation born?

The civilisation of ancient Egypt began around 5,000 years ago, with the reign of King Menes. He united Upper and Lower Egypt into one kingdom. This is believed to have begun the first Egyptian dynasty, or family of rulers, in 3100 B.C.

The Nemes headdress was a royal, blue-and-gold striped headpiece made of stiff cloth

Pharaohs wore colourful linen clothes that were decorated with beads and golden threads

Q How many dynasties ruled ancient Egypt?

About 30 dynasties ruled during the different periods of the ancient Egyptian civilisation. These periods – roughly extending from about 3100 B.C. to A.D. 395 – were the Late Predynastic Period, the Early Dynastic Period, the Old Kingdom, the First Intermediate Period, the Middle Kingdom, the Second Intermediate Period, the New Kingdom, the Third Intermediate Period, the Late Period and the Greco-Roman Period.

 Q What kind of clothes did Egyptian pharaohs wear?

Male pharaohs wore kilts made of fine linen and decorated with colourful sashes and ornaments. They wore leather sandals and carried staffs known as flails, which symbolised their power. Pharaohs also wore eye make-up and fake beards. Female pharaohs wore flowing tunics of fine cloth and lots of jewellery, make-up and decorative sandals.

 Q What powers were attributed to the pharaohs?

The ancient Egyptians identified their pharaohs with various gods, including Horus, Ra and Osiris. The pharaoh was regarded as all-knowing and all-powerful and endowed with supernatural powers. He had control over the whole country and his word was supreme!

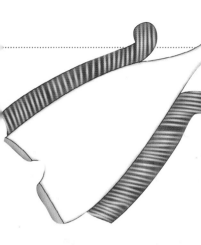

This White Crown belonged to King Osiris. Its sides were decorated with feathers

How many different types of crowns did pharaohs wear?

Pharaohs wore a variety of headdresses for different occasions. These included the Red Crown, the White Crown, the Khepresh (Blue) Crown, the Double Crown, the Atef Crown and the Nemes Headdress.

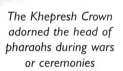

When did pharaohs wear the Khepresh Crown?

The Khepresh, or Blue, Crown, was worn by pharaohs during battles and ceremonies. These crowns were typically made of blue leather and richly decorated with ostrich feathers, gold or bronze sun disks and figures of cobras.

The Khepresh Crown adorned the head of pharaohs during wars or ceremonies

What is the difference between the Red, White and Double crowns?

The White Crown represented a king's rule in Upper Egypt, while the Red Crown symbolised rule in Lower Egypt. The Double Crown, which combined both the White and Red crowns, symbolised a pharaoh's power over both Upper and Lower Egypt.

The Double Crown of the pharaoh was the ultimate symbol of power

□ The first records of navel piercing date back to ancient Egypt. However, only pharaohs and their family members had the right to pierce their navels!

□ Ancient Egyptian rulers had decorative ceremonial palettes that were carved with images of warfare. One of the most famous palettes is the Palette of King Narmer, which belonged to the first Egyptian pharaoh, King Menes. It is believed that Narmer was another one of his names.

The Narmer Palette is a symbol of the unification of Upper and Lower Egypt. Discovered in 3200 B.C., it is carved with depictions of King Narmer's victory over his enemies

□ Egyptian pharaohs were known to eat garlic to fight against infections.

LAND OF THE PHARAOH

 Which is the best known object found in King Tutankhamun's tomb?

The most famous treasure uncovered from the royal tomb of Tutankhamun was his funerary mask. Made of gold and inlaid with precious stones, the mask was used to cover the face of the king's mummified body.

 When did the ancient Egyptian civilisation come to an end?

The end of the ancient Egyptian civilisation started around 332 B.C., with the invasion of the Egyptian empire by Alexander the Great. About 30 B.C., the people of ancient Egypt became a part of the Roman Empire.

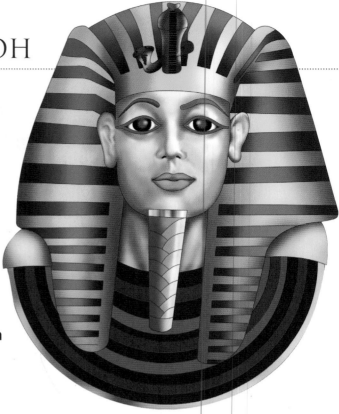

The famous mask of King Tut was made of pure gold and covered the head and shoulders of the king's mummy

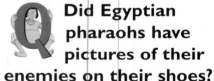 **Did Egyptian pharaohs have pictures of their enemies on their shoes?**

Ancient Egyptian pharaohs wore wooden sandals with pictures of enemies on the soles. The treading of the pharaoh in these shoes symbolised the trampling of his enemies to defeat!

Which pharaoh's wife was said to be the most beautiful woman to have ever lived in ancient Egypt?

Queen Nefertiti, the royal wife of Pharaoh Akhenaten, was said to be the most beautiful woman in the history of ancient Egypt.

The bust of Queen Nefertiti is one of the most famous icons of ancient Egypt

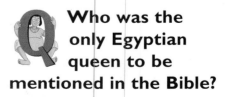 **Who was the only Egyptian queen to be mentioned in the Bible?**

Queen Tahpenes was the only Egyptian queen to find a place in the Bible. She ruled during the reigns of David and Solomon.

GODS ON EARTH

The Egyptian people worshipped many different deities as gods who lived on earth.

Animal Worship

The earliest Egyptians were known to practice animal worship. Some animals, like the cat, were considered very sacred. With time, the gods and goddesses were represented with animal heads and human bodies. This was because the Egyptians believed that their deities could appear in both human and animal forms. Goddess Bast (or Bastet), a very important deity, was represented in the form of half-woman, half-cat in sculptures. She symbolised joy, dancing and music, and health and healing.

This gold statue is of the Sacred Cat of Bast, which is associated with Goddess Bastet

Great Gods and Goddesses

The Egyptians grouped their deities in various ways. The most important grouping was the Great Ennead of Heliopolis, a council of the nine main deities of ancient Egypt – Ra (Atum), Shu, Tefnut, Geb, Nut, Osiris, Isis, Seth and Nephthys. The first five represented the five elements of nature: sun, air, moisture, earth and sky.

GODS ON EARTH

 What kind of deities did the ancient Egyptians worship?

Gods and goddesses in ancient Egypt often represented the forces of nature, such as the sun, sky, earth and wind. The people believed that their gods and goddesses lived on earth and portrayed them with human bodies and animal heads.

 Why was the decoration of coffins so important?

The ancient Egyptians believed that if coffins were not decorated, the ka of a dead person would not be able to journey between the body and the afterlife!

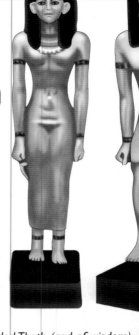

Egyptian deities included Thoth (god of wisdom), Ra (sun god), Hathor (goddess of love), Khnum (creator god) and Anubis (god of the dead)

 Who was regarded as the most important pharaoh of ancient Egypt?

Ramses II, also called Ramses the Great, was considered to be the most important pharaoh and god-king. Also known as 'Horus', 'Warrior King' and 'Son of Ra', he ruled Egypt for about 66 years, during which he fought many important wars.

Scenes of Ramses II on his war chariot have often been depicted on the tomb walls of ancient Egypt

 How was the human body classified in ancient Egyptian religion?

According to ancient Egyptian religion, the human body was divided into 36 parts. A particular god or goddess was believed to protect each of these parts.

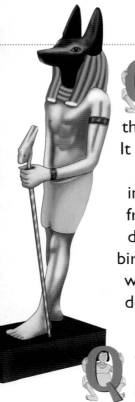

Q What were the ba and the ka?

The ba and the ka represented the spirits of the dead in ancient Egypt. It was commonly believed that everyone had a ba (soul) as well as a ka (an invisible twin). The ba and the ka were freed from the body after the person's death. The ba, which was depicted as a bird, could travel freely and kept in touch with friends and family members of the dead person. In the afterlife, the goal of the ba was to seek out the ka.

Q Who was the most important god in ancient Egypt?

The ancient Egyptians considered the sun god, Ra (or Re), as the creator of everything. He was represented with a man's body and a hawk's head. In his hand he held an ankh and a wand.

Q Which ancient Egyptian temples were moved from their original location?

In the 1960s, the temple complex in the island of Philae, in Aswan, Egypt, was moved to protect it from the rising water levels of the Nile River when the Aswan Dam was erected. The temples were put back together on the island of Agilkia.

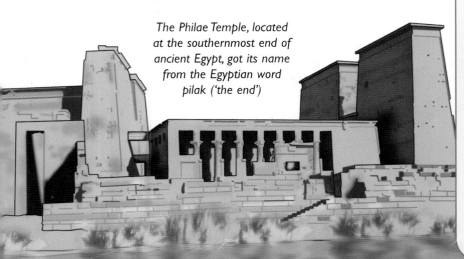

The Philae Temple, located at the southernmost end of ancient Egypt, got its name from the Egyptian word pilak ('the end')

FACT BOX

□ Ancient Egyptian tablets suggest that the people used incense sticks during prayer. These sticks were probably placed in decorated holders or stands.

The religious Egyptians burned incense sticks on holders at temples and in their homes

□ Goddess Nut was the goddess of the sky in ancient Egypt. She was represented posing on her hands and feet, stretched in the shape of an arc across the sky. Her blue-coloured body was usually shown as covered in stars.

□ An ancient Egyptian legend relates that Seth, the wicked brother of Isis and Osiris, killed Osiris and scattered his body in 14 different parts. Isis gathered the pieces and magically bound them together with strips of cloth and made the very first Egyptian mummy!

11

GODS ON EARTH

 In what state was the temple of Horus at Edfu discovered?

The temple at Edfu was almost entirely buried under the desert sands until the time it was discovered. Not surprisingly, it remains one of the best-preserved temples of ancient Egypt. It was built between 237 B.C. and 57 B.C. for Horus, the falcon-headed god.

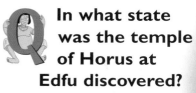

The Edfu Temple is regarded as the best-preserved temple of ancient Egypt

 Which ancient Egyptian statue represented the sun god?

In ancient Egypt, statues of the sphinx represented the sun god, with the facial features of the reigning pharaoh. The sphinx, a figure of a male lion with a human head, symbolised infinite wisdom.

What leads up to the entrance of the Luxor Temple in Egypt?

The entrance to the Luxor Temple is lined with a row of over 60 sphinxes! The temple was built during the 18th dynasty to honour the god Amun.

What is the *Book of the Dead*?

The *Book of the Dead* is a collection of religious and magical literature written in ancient Egypt. The ancient Egyptians knew it as *The Chapter of Coming-Forth-by-Day*. Copies of this book, in the form of papyrus scrolls, were placed inside the tombs of important people.

What was the *menat*?

The *menat* was a beaded collar or necklace that was believed to have derived healing powers from the goddess Hathor.

The remains of an ancient church and and an Islamic mosque were discovered at the Luxor Temple

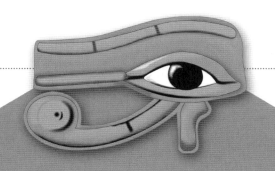

BELIEFS AND CUSTOMS

Ancient Egyptian rituals were based on people's faith in the gods, pharaohs, animal worship and the forces of nature.

Life and Death

Central to Egyptian religion was the belief in life after death. The soul moved on to a new world after leaving the body. It was thought that the god Osiris carried the body across the Nile into the afterlife.

Might of Magic

The Egyptians perceived the influence of magic in every aspect of life, from social customs to the practice of medicine. Their belief in an eternal life was depicted in several charms. The key-shaped ankh – resembling a T-shaped cross with a loop over it – represented health and happiness.

The ancient Egyptians had their share of unusual beliefs as well. One was that frogs and worms came from the deposits of the Nile River's floods! The black colour of the Nile's mineral-rich soil even led the people to believe that black was a lucky colour. Probably the strangest of their beliefs was that headaches and toothaches could be cured by eating fried mice!

The ankh, a symbol of eternal life in ancient Egypt, means 'life' in the Egyptian language

BELIEFS AND CUSTOMS

 How was religion related to the beliefs and customs of ancient Egypt?

Egyptian beliefs and customs revolved around religion. The people worshipped nearly 2,000 deities, in the form of idols at temples and shrines. It is said that people were only allowed up to the entrance of these temples, but conveyed messages to the gods through priests, who were regarded as servants of the gods.

In ancient Egypt, a temple was the 'house of god' and the god lived in idol form inside a shrine or a sanctuary

 Why were scribes given a high status in the society?

Scribes were the only ones in Egypt who could read and write, so they enjoyed a high status in society. They could perform many different tasks, like writing letters, keeping accounts and maintaining important records.

How was the social status of an ancient Egyptian decided?

A person's position in ancient Egyptian society was decided by the job he did. Thus, among the various classes were soldiers, farmers, craftsmen, engineers, priests and noblemen.

What kind of ancient Egyptian objects were thought to have magical qualities?

The people of ancient Egypt believed that amulets, or charms, had magical powers. Amulets were considered to bring good luck and health and protect against evil forces.

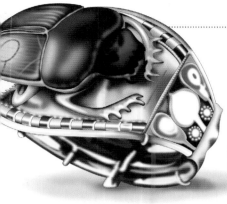

The Egyptians called the scarab beetle 'Kheper'

 Which was the most popular Egyptian amulet?

The most common amulet in ancient Egypt was that of the scarab beetle. The scarab was the spiritual symbol of the god Ra. It represented eternal life.

Q **What did the custom of *inw* involve?**

The *inw* was an important Egyptian custom of exchanging gifts between people of different social statuses.

Q **What were the different social classes of ancient Egypt?**

The social structure of ancient Egypt was like a pyramid. At the base was the majority of the population, comprising soldiers, farmers and tomb builders. Higher up were the skilled craftsmen and above them were the scribes. Still higher were priests, doctors and engineers.

Close to the top were high priests and noblemen, followed by the vizier, or the pharaoh's advisor. Finally, at the head was the pharaoh.

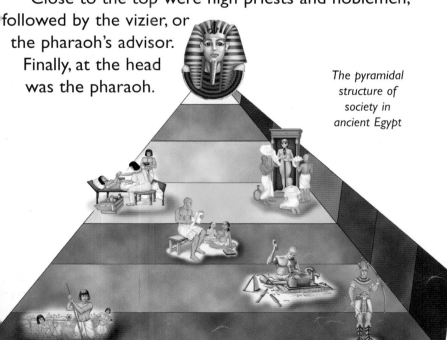
The pyramidal structure of society in ancient Egypt

❑ According to an ancient Egyptian belief, shadows were one of the important elements that humans were made of. The shadow was thought to protect a person from harm.

❑ Special flasks were exchanged as gifts during New Year's Eve celebrations in ancient Egypt. These New Year flasks had inscriptions that were said to summon the gods, to bless the owners of the flasks with a healthy and happy life in the new year.

New Year flasks in ancient Egypt were filled with water from a sacred pool

❑ Egyptian marriages were not elaborate ceremonies. Two people were considered to be 'married' when they moved into a common household together.

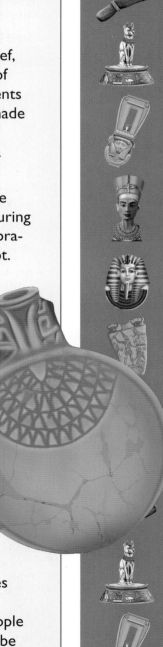

BELIEFS AND CUSTOMS

 What is the Eye of Horus?

The Eye of Horus was the name of a common ancient Egyptian symbol. Also known as the 'magic eye' or the *udjat*, it represented the eye of the god Horus. The eye featured commonly on amulets and was believed to be a powerful symbol that protected people from evil and guided them along the right path.

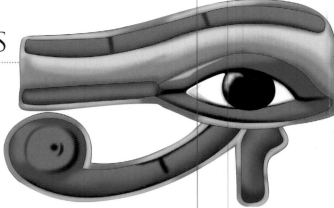

Different parts of the Eye of Horus stood for fractions in mathematics, with the complete eye representing the value of '1'!

 How did the ancient Egyptians cure illnesses?

According to the ancient Egyptians, illnesses were caused by angry gods or evil spirits that entered a person's body. Doctors and priests would use their knowledge and powers to get rid of illnesses. Their cures included amulets, magic spells and various potions.

What special association do wedding rings have with ancient Egypt?

The custom of wearing an engagement ring on the fourth finger of the left hand is said to have come from ancient Egypt. The Egyptians believed that the vein running from that particular finger was directly connected to the heart!

 How did Egyptian pharaohs keep from getting drunk?

It is said that ancient Egyptian pharaohs ate lots of cabbage before they drank alcohol. They believed that this would allow them to drink without any side effects!

 Did ancient Egyptians marry their siblings?

Ancient Egyptians were known to marry people they were related to. However, it was also common for unrelated couples to call each other 'brother' or 'sister' affectionately!

In ancient Egypt, the bride was usually 14-15 years old and the groom, around 17!

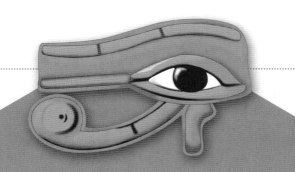

MUMMY MAGIC!

An interesting feature of the Egyptian civilisation was the elaborate rituals that followed from the peopl's faith in the afterlife.

Making Mummies

Ancient Egyptians took great care to preserve dead bodies, to aid the passage to the next world. They used a process called embalming, or mummification.

The body was first cleaned with salts, oils, wines and spices and left to dry. Body parts were removed, dried and then stored separately in canopic jars. These jars were meant to call upon the protection of guardian gods, each for one organ. The jars were placed inside a canopic chest.

Finally, the body was wrapped carefully in linen bandages, with amulets placed in between the layers and placed in a coffin, which was buried inside a tomb.

Canopic jars had lids in the shape of human, baboon, falcon and jackal heads, symbolising the spirits of the four sons of Horus

Tomb Talk

The poor people were usually buried in ordinary, small coffins made of reed. Grand tombs were reserved for the royalty and other important people.

MUMMY MAGIC!

 What did the process of evisceration involve?

Before a dead body was wrapped up, all internal organs except the heart were removed. This process was known as evisceration.

 Which chemical was used for drying and preserving the body?

A salt deposit extracted from dried-up river beds was used to dry and cleanse dead bodies. It was known as natron.

 When did the ancient Egyptians begin to make mummies?

The ancient Egyptians started mummifying the bodies of royal and important people sometime in about 2400 B.C. The practice continued for nearly 3,000 years.

What were linen strips, used for wrapping mummies, sometimes soaked in?

The linen strips used to wrap dead bodies were sometimes soaked in plaster to quicken the drying process.

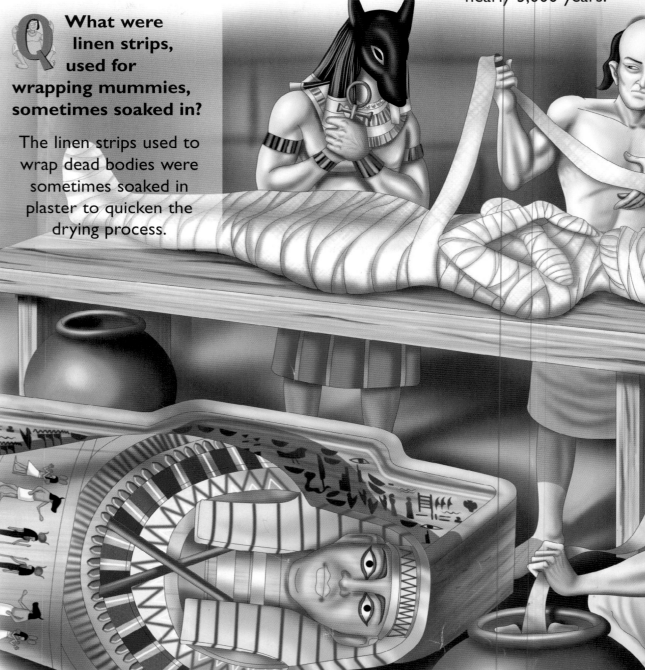

Why did ancient Egyptians bury the bodies of dead people in pyramids?

Ancient Egyptians believed that preserving the body of a dead person would enable him to live comfortably in the afterlife. Therefore, they built elaborate pyramids to bury their dead.

How did the process of mummification come about?

The process of mummificatian lasted nearly two months!

The Egyptians thought of using mummification after they realised that the hot sands of the deserts and the surrounding climate dried up corpses, instead of turning them to dust.

Who were the people involved in mummification?

Mummification was a religious ceremony in ancient Egypt and was performed by priests. One of the priests used to wear the jackal-shaped mask of Anubis, the god of the dead.

The funeral barges of ancient Egyptian pharaohs were also called 'sun boats'

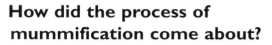

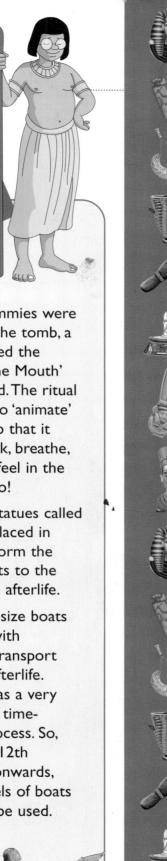

FACT BOX

□ Before mummies were placed inside the tomb, a ceremony called the 'Opening of the Mouth' was performed. The ritual was believed to 'animate' the mummy so that it could eat, drink, breathe, see, hear and feel in the next world too!

□ Miniature statues called *shabti*s were placed in tombs to perform the role of servants to the mummy in the afterlife.

□ Initially, full-size boats were buried with mummies to transport them to the afterlife. However, it was a very expensive and time-consuming process. So, from the 12th Dynasty onwards, tiny models of boats began to be used.

MUMMY MAGIC!

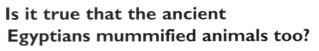

Q **What kind of objects was buried along with the mummy?**

Day-to-day objects and precious belongings were buried along with the mummy, so that he would have all he might need in the next life. Many treasures were found inside Tutankhamun's tomb, among them his gold scabbard and dagger, golden throne and jewellery chest.

Q **Is it true that the ancient Egyptians mummified animals too?**

Hundreds of mummified crocodiles, cats, snakes and other creatures have been found in Egypt. Some pets were buried alongside their mummified owners, while others were preserved because they were held sacred.

King Tut's dagger, made of gold, glass and precious stones, was found attached to the waist of his mummified body

The Egyptians used to mummify dogs as well and placed them at the feet of their owners!

Q **Why was the heart the only organ left inside the dead body?**

The Egyptians held that the heart, rather than the brain, was the most important organ. They considered it to be the source of all thoughts, feelings and intelligence. In fact, the heart was thought to testify for the dead person in the afterlife! This is why the Egyptians left the heart intact.

Q **How were organs removed from the body?**

The brain was pulled out through the nostrils with a metal hook and then thrown away. Other organs like the liver, lungs, stomach and intestines were usually removed by making an opening near the stomach, after which they were preserved in canopic jars.

Q **Is it true that only the bodies of royal people were mummified?**

At first, only Egyptian kings were mummified and buried inside royal pyramids. According to ancient legend, Osiris was the first Egyptian mummy. Later, common people also began to be mummified.

DAILY LIFE

The day-to-day life in ancient Egypt was not very different from the way people live today.

Family Values

The Egyptians highly valued their family life. They worked during the day and played games and listened to music in their free time. The father earned the livelihood, while the mother looked after the children and the home. The rich had servants to attend to the daily chores. People also kept pets such as cats and monkeys.

School Stories

Only rich families sent their boys to schools, which were called 'houses of instruction'. There they were taught by the learned scribes. They used papyrus paper, reed brushes and ink made from black soot and water. Girls did not go to school, but learnt music, dancing and household skills at home.

Egyptian students were taught hieroglyphs as well as mathematics and record-keeping. They wrote on ostraca (pieces of pottery) because papyrus was too costly to practice on

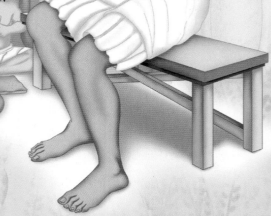

DAILY LIFE

The hand-operated shaduf was one of the earliest devices invented for water irrigation

What was the *shaduf*?

The *shaduf* was an irrigation device invented by the Egyptians for lifting water. It was made up of a long pole, which was held steady by a post stuck upright into the ground. A weight and a bucket hung from either end of the pole. The bucket would be lowered down to the water and lifted back with the help of the weight. By turning the pole, the bucket was then emptied into an irrigation channel.

The economy of ancient Egypt was largely based on farming and the people spent much of their time on farming activities

Were the ancient Egyptians bald?

Most ancient Egyptians, both men and women, had their hair shaven regularly and wore wigs instead! These wigs, made of human hair or sheep's wool, kept the shaved heads both warm and free from lice. The priests even shaved their entire bodies as further safeguard against lice!

Were houses in ancient Egypt decorated indoors?

The houses of rich Egyptian families had decorative wall paintings, coloured ceilings and tiled floors. Poorer homes were simple, with floors of beaten earth and hardly any decoration.

Was farming a major activity in ancient Egypt?

The economy of ancient Egypt was based on farming. Most of the people were farmers and they spent a large part of the year raising cattle and growing crops. Part of these crops was given to the pharaoh as tax.

Q Did people in ancient Egypt wear make-up?

Both men and women in ancient Egypt took great care of their personal appearance and wore a variety of make-up. They painted their eyes, lips and cheeks, using cosmetics made from natural, coloured minerals mixed with water and oil.

Q How important was the Nile River to the ancient Egyptians?

Most ancient Egyptians lived along the Nile, which provided them with water for drinking, bathing and agriculture. People transported crops, cattle and building materials in boats and barges on the Nile.

Q What kind of tools did farmers in ancient Egypt use?

The farmers used hand tools like hoes, ploughs, sickles, forks and scoops. Later, the *shaduf* and the waterwheel were used to irrigate the crops.

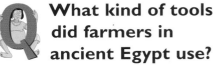

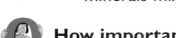

The Egyptians wove sandals made of the reed plant

FACT BOX

□ The ancient Egyptians devised the nilometre to measure the water level of the Nile during floods. The nilometre was a kind of staircase going down into the Nile. It had marks on its sides to indicate the level of the river water.

□ The common people of ancient Egypt ate out of clay dishes, while the rich were served on bronze, silver and gold plates. The rich could also afford to drink wine, which was very expensive. Other people drank beer.

□ People in ancient Egypt wore sandals only for special occasions, or when they felt the need. These sandals were made by stitching woven leather or reed. Rich people wore decorative sandals of leather and even of gold.

DAILY LIFE

Did the ancient Egyptians buy things with money?

In ancient Egypt, people got their goods through exchange, instead of buying them with money. This was called barter. Goods were weighed on scales and exchanged with grains amounting to either the same weight or value.

What kind of clothes were common in ancient Egypt?

The usual clothing for men was a loincloth or a kilt, while that for women was a simple dress held with straps. Royal and important people wore beaded dresses and decorative robes made of high-quality linen.

How did ancient Egyptians clean their homes?

Ancient Egyptians usually cleaned their houses with brushes made of natural materials like tree fibres and reed.

The ancient Egyptians used grass and reed brooms

Did the Egyptians use pillows?

In ancient Egypt, people did not use pillows. Instead, they used wooden or stone headrests. These were U-shaped supports believed to have been covered with cloth for cushioning.

What kind of houses did the ancient Egyptians live in?

Most people in ancient Egypt lived in adobe houses. These were made of sun-baked mud bricks, straws and pebbles. The poor lived in single-room homes. The better-off classes had double-storey houses with at least two or three rooms. The rich homes had as many as 10 rooms.

Most people in ancient Egypt led simple lives in their adobe homes. They slept on wooden cots and headrests. The women looked after the house, baked bread and groomed themselves, while the children played with toys

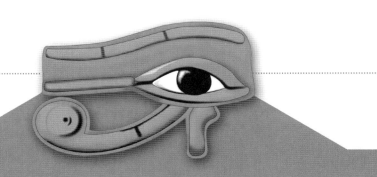

ARTS AND CRAFTS

Did you know that there was no specific word for 'artist' in the ancient Egyptian language? Even so, art played an important role in everything, from religious duties to daily activities.

The Skilled Ones

Egyptian craftsmen usually learned their skills from their fathers. They were well-respected in society. Religious objects, made for temples and pharaohs, were made in special workshops inside the temple or the royal palace. Other items were crafted at smaller workshops.

Creative Crafts

Potters shaped vessels by hand and glazed them, before hardening them in fire. Goldsmiths crafted artistic jewellery, daily objects, statues and coffins, while sculptors carved beautiful statues, artefacts and monuments.

The skilled Egyptian sculptors carved statues to honor kings and queens, decorated temple walls and crafted artefacts and other daily objects

ARTS AND CRAFTS

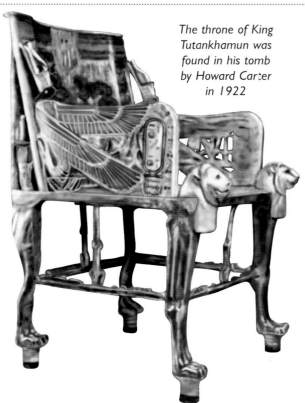

The throne of King Tutankhamun was found in his tomb by Howard Carter in 1922

Q **Were the thrones of Egyptian pharaohs richly decorated?**

The thrones of Egyptian pharaohs were usually crafted with precious metals and stones. King Tutankhamun's throne was made of wood and coated with pure gold. It was inlaid with a blue stone called faience and other semi-precious stones.

Q **What kind of art was created in ancient Egypt?**

Arts and crafts in ancient Egypt included textile and fibre weaving, tent making, papyrus craft, metal and stone sculpting, jewellery making and wall painting.

Q **Which metals did Egyptian craftsmen use to make jewellery?**

Egyptian craftsmen used copper and gold to make jewellery as well as statues. These were the earliest metals found in ancient Egypt. Excavated tombs from that time have revealed exquisite gold earrings, necklaces and neck collars.

These gold earrings, depicting birds with heads of ducks and wings of falcons, belonged to King Tut

Q **What was the main purpose of art in ancient Egypt?**

The ancient Egyptians usually created art for religious rituals. All forms of Egyptian art had special meanings and roles in religion as well as for the afterlife.

The Egyptians believed that wearing amulets and charms on their jewellery would protect them from evil

Q **What kind of decoration was often seen on ancient Egyptian jewellery?**

Ancient Egyptian jewellery was often decorated with amulets. The people of ancient Egypt strongly believed in charms, so they wore bangles, necklaces and rings with amulet designs.

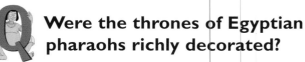

How were clothes made in ancient Egypt?

Clothes were made by weaving linen threads produced from the fibre of the flax plant. Usually women worked on the spinning looms.

Weaving in ancient Egypt was done mainly on hand-operated looms

Intricately carved ivory combs were often placed inside the tombs of royal mummies

Which well-known technique related to pottery was invented by the ancient Egyptians?

The art of coating pottery with enamel was invented in ancient Egypt. Sculptors used hand-operated potter's wheels to make clay dishes, which were used for cooking, eating, drinking and storing things.

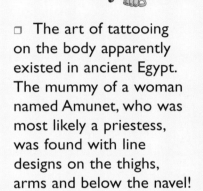

FACT BOX

□ The art of tattooing on the body apparently existed in ancient Egypt. The mummy of a woman named Amunet, who was most likely a priestess, was found with line designs on the thighs, arms and below the navel!

□ The world's first man-made pigment is said to be Egyptian blue, probably created as an offshoot of the manufacture of blue-glazed stones called faience. The colour is made by grinding up a compound made when sand is melted together with copper minerals and chalk.

□ Ivory and bone were used extensively in making small objects such as beads, needles and combs.

ARTS AND CRAFTS

 What kind of tools did ancient Egyptian craftsmen use?

Ancient Egyptian artists used many different tools of stone, wood and metal. These included saws, bow drills, axes, chisels, awls, adzes, winnowing fans and sickles. Chips of limestone and broken pottery, known as ostraca, were commonly used as pads for draft sketches.

 Did artists have rules for using different colours based on gender?

There were strict rules for using colours. Artists used only reddish-brown shades for colouring men's skin. Women figures were coloured in shades of yellow and at times in pink too!

 Why were sculptures placed inside tombs?

Sculptures of all types and sizes were placed inside the tombs of the dead in ancient Egypt. Sculptures were seen as homes for the mummy's spirit, or gifts to a deity.

 Where did ancient Egyptian painters get their colours from?

Egyptian artists made their own colours by grinding natural materials like mineral rocks. Commonly used colours included black, white, grey, red, blue, green, pink and yellow.

 Why did ancient Egyptian artists paint the walls of tombs?

The Egyptians believed that paintings and relief images on tomb walls assured the dead person's survival in the afterlife. They often showed scenes from the life of the dead person.

One of the most important jobs of ancient Egyptian artists was painting the walls of royal tombs

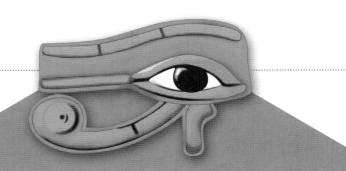

ARCHITECTURE

Ancient Egyptian architecture, too, was influenced by religion. This is why the most elaborate structures were the temples and the pyramids.

Princely Pyramids

The Egyptians built pyramids to bury their pharaohs. Initially, single-level, square-shaped tombs (mastabas) were built, with just enough room for the coffin.

Later, the Egyptians built a series of steps on top of the mastabas, leading up to a flat-topped platform. These were the first proper pyramids and were called step pyramids. The steps were believed to guide the dead to the heavens.

Still later, the steps were filled in to smoothen the sides. The Egyptians thought that the sunrays would reflect off the smooth sides to form a ramp leading to heaven! The most famous of these cone-shaped pyramids are the three Pyramids of Giza. One of these, the Khufu Pyramid, is the oldest standing structure among the Seven Wonders of the World! It was built for King Khufu over 4,000 years ago,

The earliest mastabas were made of mud brick, while the later ones were of stone, or stone-covered clay bricks

ARCHITECTURE

 Which kind of architectural column was common in ancient Egypt?

Columns depicting the image of Hathor on the capital were commonly used in ancient Egyptian architecture. These columns were decorated with the sculpted head of Hathor, the goddess of love, joy and motherhood.

Columns featured prominently in the architecture of Egyptian temples

Ancient Egyptians used basic tools to cut, carve and shape building materials

 What kind of tools were used to construct pyramids and temples?

The Egyptians used a number of tools for building pyramids and temples. Granite hammers, metal chisels, pickaxes and other strong tools were used to cut and carve hard stone blocks. Right angles and plumb lines were used to ensure that the sides of the stone blocks were in a straight line.

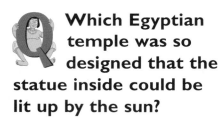 **Which Egyptian temple was so designed that the statue inside could be lit up by the sun?**

The gigantic Temple of Ramses II at Abu Simbel, which houses a big statue of Ramses II, was so designed that the sunrays could enter the inner sanctuary twice a year and light up the statue.

 Were Egyptian temples made to look like plants?

The pillars and columns of Egyptian temples were often carved to look like palm trees, papyrus reeds and lotus plants.

The Great Pyramid of Giza is among the Seven Wonders of the Ancient World

 Which was the first pyramid built in ancient Egypt?

The first known Egyptian pyramid was the Step Pyramid of King Zoser (Djoser), at Saqqara. Built nearly 5,000 years ago by the architect Imhotep, it was the biggest stone structure of its time.

How many people were needed to build a single pyramid?

Thousands of workers and artists were involved in the construction of a single pyramid. This often included more than 4,000 craftsmen and stonemasons, as well as farmers who worked mainly so that they could pay off their taxes.

 Which is the largest stone structure in the world?

The Great Pyramid at Giza is the world's largest stone structure. Nearly 140 m (459 feet) tall, it is made up of more than 2 million blocks of limestone! The pyramid is famous for the massive Great Sphinx statue that guards it. It is believed to be amongst the largest sculptures ever.

FACT BOX

❏ Imhotep of Egypt is considered to be the first known architect. He built the complex of King Netjerikhet (Djoser) at Saqqara.

❏ Pyramid workers commonly carried water bottles made of animal hide.

A water container made from animal hide

❏ There are over 90 pyramids in Egypt. The last one was built in 1570 B.C. Pyramids were found to be easily accessible to robbers. From the New Kingdom onwards, pharaohs and their treasures were buried in tombs carved in cliffs, which lay hidden in a valley.

ARCHITECTURE

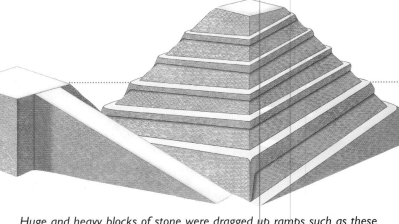

 Did workers actually lift stone blocks while building pyramids?

Pyramid workers could not have lifted such heavy blocks of stone on their own. Historians believe that sloping ramps were erected around the sides of the pyramid, somewhat like a stairway. The stone blocks were then placed on wooden sledges and pulled up the ramps by ropes.

Huge and heavy blocks of stone were dragged up ramps such as these

Why did the Egyptians build pyramids only on the west bank of the Nile River?

Since the sun set on the west bank of the Nile, the ancient Egyptians believed that this was the 'land of the dead'. They, therefore, built the pyramids on the west bank, while building their own houses on the east bank, the point of sunrise.

 Were buildings and structures in ancient Egypt decorative?

In ancient Egypt, pyramids, palaces and temples were decorated with rich hieroglyphics, drawings and paintings. Hieroglyphs ('sacred carvings') were commonly used to carve pictures on walls. of temples and pyramids.

What materials were the pyramids of ancient Egypt made of?

Pyramids were built with massive slabs of different stones. Rough limestone was used for the main structure, while a finer, white limestone was used for casing the outer layer as well as the inner walls. Often, pink granite covered the walls inside. Basalt and alabaster were occasionally used for the floors.

The merkhet was invented by the Egyptians sometime around 600 B.C.

 What role did the stars play in the building of Egyptian pyramids?

The ancient Egyptians built their pyramids and temples according to the pattern of stars in the sky. They used astrological tools like the *merkhet* ('instrument of knowing') to do this. Made from the rib of a palm tree leaf, the merkhet is said to be the earliest astronomical tool in the world.

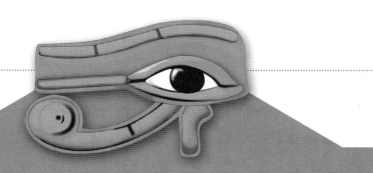

GAMES AND ENTERTAINMENT

The people of ancient Egypt found different ways to entertain themselves in their free time.

Sporting Spirit

It is believed that the ancient Egyptians invented the sport of fencing (performed with blunt swords). Tomb drawings have also shown people playing with sticks made of palm-tree branches that resemble hockey sticks and a ball made of papyrus fibres. The Egyptians devised proper rules for their games and even had referees, player uniforms and prizes!

Popular sports included running, swimming, wrestling, weightlifting, boxing, archery and rowing. Many of these were practiced for fitness.

Huntsman's Instinct

Egyptian men enjoyed hunting. Pharaohs held hunting to be a symbol of bravery. Hunting was also a way of getting meat for food. Animal bones, feathers, horns, leather and shells were used to make such items as clothes, jewellery and religious objects.

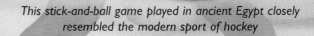

This stick-and-ball game played in ancient Egypt closely resembled the modern sport of hockey

GAMES AND ENTERTAINMENT

The very popular game of senet was played by both the rich and the poor

 Which popular game played in ancient Egypt resembled the game of chess?

Senet was the national game in ancient Egypt for about 3,000 years. It was a board game, somewhat like chess and backgammon, played by both royal and common people. The objective of the two-player game was to move along the triple rows of squares or 'houses' (each of which held mystic qualities) and get their 7 pieces off the board completely.

Which ancient Egyptian game was named after two types of animals?

An ancient Egyptian board game called 'Dogs and Jackals' featured four animal legs and a palm tree with about 55 holes carved on it. The game consisted of five counters for each player, with three coins that determined the movement of these counters. The person who first managed to move all his counters up the palm tree was the winner.

 What was the 'Tug of Hoop'?

The 'Tug of Hoop' was a game played in ancient Egypt. Two people competed by pulling a common hoop towards themselves with a hooked stick. The players were not allowed to let the hoop fall flat on to the ground.

Music and dance were integral to any occasion or festival in ancient Egypt

Children in ancient Egypt played outdoor games like 'khuzza lawiizza' (leap frog), tug of war, handball and wrestling

How did ancient Egyptian children amuse hemselves?

Children in ancient Egypt played games like leap frog, hopscotch and goose step. Ball games were another popular pastime. Children also played with different kinds of toys.

How was the ancient Egyptian sport of high jumping played?

Two people sat facing each other and stretched their legs out to create a jumping barrier. A third person had to jump over the barrier. The barrier could be increased by putting their palms over their feet. The third player would then attempt to jump without touching the barrier! The game is still played in parts of Egypt and is known as 'goose steps'.

What kind of musical instruments were played in ancient Egypt?

The ancient Egyptians played string instruments like harps and lyres, wind instruments such as clarinets, flutes, oboes and lutes, and percussions like drums, tambourines and cymbals.

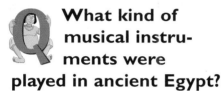

Who danced and played music at festivals and banquets?

Women from poorer families in ancient Egypt usually danced or played at important festivals and banquets.

☐ The Dance of the Muu was a special dance performed by men during ancient Egyptian funerals. The dancers wore head-dresses made of reeds.

☐ The sistrum was an ancient Egyptian musical rattle. It was often played by women musicians in temples. Its sound was said to drive away evil powers!

A set of rings on the sacred sistrum created a rattling sound against metal crossbars

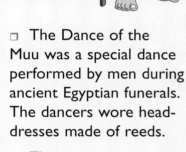

☐ It is believed that the first form of the musical pipe organ was invented in ancient Egypt.

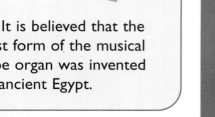
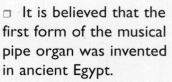
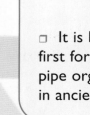

GAMES AND ENTERTAINMENT

 Were the ancient Egyptians good at gymnastics?

Ancient Egyptian gymnasts were skilled at performing complicated moves. Take the consecutive vault, for instance. This involved turning in mid-air more than once, without touching their heads on the ground! When finished, they would land to stand absolutely straight, which is still a gymnastics rule in the modern Olympics.

The Egyptians performed gymnastic exercises to keep themselves fit and strong

 Is the oldest document of sports recorded in Egypt?

The oldest document relating to sports is in the form of a mural painting in ancient Egypt. It shows the great pharaoh, Zoser the Great, participating in a running event during the Heb Sed Festival.

 Was the earliest record of bowling really discovered in Egypt?

The very first record of bowling has been dated to ancient Egypt, some 7,000 years back. A round object resembling the modern bowling ball and long marble bars that looked like bowling pins were discovered inside an ancient pyramid ruin.

 Did people in ancient Egypt have feasts and festivals?

The ancient Egyptians held a variety of feasts and festivals. Festivals were usually celebrated for religious purposes, in honour of the gods and goddesses. The greatest number of festivals took place during the flood season.

The Egyptians used nets, hooks and harpoons to catch fish. The earliest hooks were made out of animal bones, but later metal hooks were used

 How do we know that the ancient Egyptians practiced fishing?

In ancient Egypt, fishing was a sport as well as a means of livelihood. Drawings on tomb walls show fishing scenes that inform us how people caught and consumed fish.

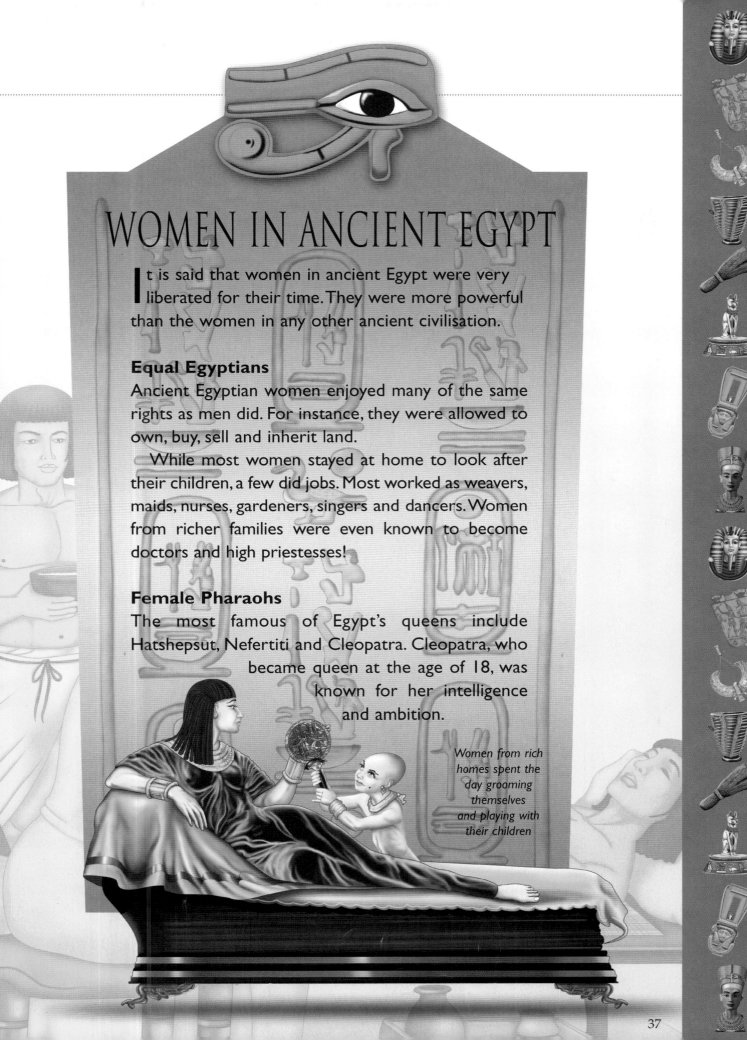

WOMEN IN ANCIENT EGYPT

It is said that women in ancient Egypt were very liberated for their time. They were more powerful than the women in any other ancient civilisation.

Equal Egyptians

Ancient Egyptian women enjoyed many of the same rights as men did. For instance, they were allowed to own, buy, sell and inherit land.

While most women stayed at home to look after their children, a few did jobs. Most worked as weavers, maids, nurses, gardeners, singers and dancers. Women from richer families were even known to become doctors and high priestesses!

Female Pharaohs

The most famous of Egypt's queens include Hatshepsut, Nefertiti and Cleopatra. Cleopatra, who became queen at the age of 18, was known for her intelligence and ambition.

Women from rich homes spent the day grooming themselves and playing with their children

 How much gold jewellery was found inside King Tutankhamun's tomb?

More than 5,000 articles of gold jewellery were discovered inside King Tut's tomb. The boy-king's mummified body itself contained nearly 150 pieces of gold jewellery. In addition, there were gold finger covers, necklaces, collars and rings. A falcon-headed collar found on the mummy was made up of about 250 pieces of gold!

The rich gold collar of King Tutankhamun

What did people in ancient Egypt use for mixing cosmetics?

The ancient Egyptian people used cosmetic spoons and palettes to mix colours, oils and ointments. The spoons were often in the shape of a female figure.

The Egyptians mixed and applied make-up with decorative cosmetic spoons of wood or metal

 How did the ancient Egyptians shave?

Tomb excavations have revealed that the ancient Egyptians used both gold and copper razors to shave. The razors dating back to the 4th century B.C. were usually kept inside leather cases

The ancient Egyptian doctors were very advanced for their time. They treated injuries and cured illnesses with the use of natural oils and plant extracts. Honey was commonly used to treat wounds

 Did the ancient Egyptians have a name for their parties?

Any party held in ancient Egypt was referred to as a 'house of beer'!

 How did the ancient Egyptians remove infections from the ear?

The ancient Egyptians invented a method called 'ear candling' to remove infections from the ear. They inserted one end of a cone-shaped, hollow candle into the ear cavity and then lighted the other end. The smoke from the candle pulled out all the extra wax and germs from the ear!

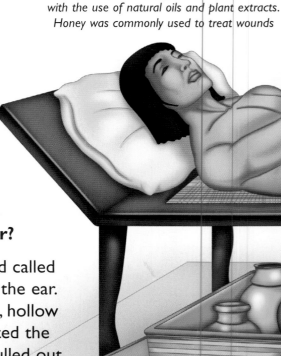

Q: What did ancient Egyptian pyramid workers eat for strength?

Workmen at pyramid sites were made to eat onions for strength! The ancient Egyptians believed that vegetables such as onion and garlic were good for health.

Q: How did Egyptian doctors maintain hygiene while treating injuries and wounds?

Egyptian doctors understood the importance of hygiene and disinfected their hands and surgical tools before treating anyone. They soaked bandages and plasters with herbs to quicken the healing process.

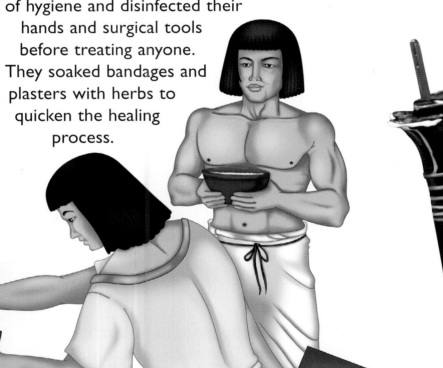

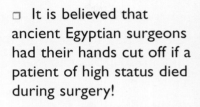

FACT BOX

□ It is believed that ancient Egyptian surgeons had their hands cut off if a patient of high status died during surgery!

□ The earliest references to the use of eye make-up date back to ancient Egypt. Both men and women painted their eyes with kohl – an eyeliner meant to make their eyes look bigger as well as to protect themselves from evil. Kohl was usually stored in long, decorative tubes and small pots.

Small and thin sticks were dipped into the cylindrical tubes to apply kohl on the eyes

□ Although the Egyptians invented glass, mirrors in ancient Egypt were not made of glass. The Egyptians did not know how to make clear glass. So they used such metals as polished bronze and silver.

EXTRAORDINARY EGYPT!

 Is the world's oldest bakery situated in ancient Egypt?

In the year 2002, what is believed to be the oldest bakery in the world was discovered at Giza. The bakery, which is over 4,000 years old, showed that the ancient Egyptians baked bread in large, bell-shaped pots called *bedja*s.

 How did the ancient Egyptians make perfume?

Egyptian perfumes were made from plant roots, leaves and flowers. Extracts from henna, cinnamon, iris, rose, lily and almond were soaked in either turpentine oil or animal fats and some-times even cooked!

The Egyptians made perfume flasks to carry and store oils and perfumes

 What did ancient Egyptian warriors wear?

Common soldiers in ancient Egypt wore white linen kilts, leather footwear and white headdresses. They carried bows and arrows. Pharaohs, who also often fought wars, wore colourful clothes and headdresses.

 What did people in ancient Egypt do if their cats died?

It is believed that people in ancient Egypt would shave their eyebrows in order to mourn the deaths of their cats!

 Why did the ancient Egyptians place cones on top of their heads?

People in ancient Egypt often attached a cone of wax or animal fat to their heads and wigs. The cone was perfumed with herbs and spices. As it gradually melted, the perfume on it would spread all over the person's body and clothes!

In ancient Egypt, kings and soldiers often fought battles together

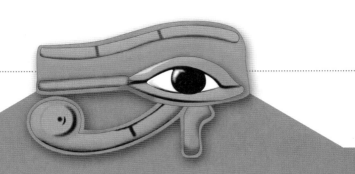

INVENTIONS AND DISCOVERIES

Ancient Egypt was the birthplace of amazing discoveries in many fields, including science, medicine, mathematics, language and writing. Perhaps this is why it is referred to as the 'cradle of civilisation'!

Time Tales

It was the Egyptians who discovered timekeeping. They kept track of time with upright stone columns called Cleopatra's Needles. The Egyptians divided the day into 12 parts, which were represented by 12 marks on the ground. As sunlight progressed during the day, the length of the column's shadow changed. The shadow's length and position on the ground showed how much daylight, or time, was left!

Medical Magic!

The Egyptian physicians were among the first to use anaesthesia. They could also fix damaged faces by using artificial noses and ears! The Egyptians had also uncovered the healing powers of flowers, herbs and animals for treating injuries and infections.

This ancient Egyptian obelisk was shifted to London, England, in 1819

INVENTIONS AND DISCOVERIES

 Was bread invented in ancient Egypt?

The ancient Egyptians are widely believed to have invented leavened (raised) bread, which was also their most common food. Dried grains such as wheat or barley were baked in clay ovens to make loaves of bread. Pharaohs and priests had bread made with fruit and honey. It is said that during the New Kingdom, there were about 40 different types of bread!

 Was the first type of paper invented in ancient Egypt?

The first form of paper was created in ancient Egypt. Sometime in 4000 B.C., the Egyptians invented writing sheets from a river plant called papyrus, which served as a strong parchment. In fact, the word 'paper' comes from 'papyrus'.

Priests and pharmacists process and record the techniques of making medicines inside a temple room

 How did the ancient Egyptians contribute to the field of medicine?

The Egyptians uncovered the causes of various diseases and developed medicinal cures for them. The first medical documents are said to be the *Ebers Papyrus*, which recorded ways to make over 800 cures.

Which drink did the ancient Egyptians invent?

The ancient Egyptians invented beer. They made it from the crumbs of lightly baked bread loaves. The crumbs were soaked in water and the mixture was fermented in huge containers to produce beer.

Beer was the most common drink in ancient Egypt. It is believed that the Egyptians flavoured their beer with date juice and honey!

Did the ancient Egyptians practice navel piercing?

The ancient Egyptians are said to have been the first to pierce their belly buttons! However, only royal or important people are believed to have been allowed to wear jewellery on the navel. If the common people did so, they were supposedly punished with death.

Was the ancient Egyptian calendar any different from the modern one?

The ancient Egyptians were the first to devise the 365-day calendar. It consisted of 12 months and 3 seasons. However, a week was made up of 10 days, while a month had just 3 weeks! The last five days in the year were observed as the birthdays of their deities, namely Osiris, Horus, Seth, Isis and Nephthys.

How did the ancient Egyptians make paper from the papyrus plant?

Strips cut from the plant's root were placed side by side with a second layer on top at a right angle. This was soaked in water and pressed under a heavy rock. The sap acted like glue and bonded it together. The outcome was a sheet which was hammered flat and dried in the sun.

FACT BOX

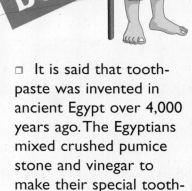

□ It is said that toothpaste was invented in ancient Egypt over 4,000 years ago. The Egyptians mixed crushed pumice stone and vinegar to make their special tooth-cleaning paste.

□ It is believed that the Egyptians invented the mathematical concepts of geometry, trigonometry and algebra.

□ The ancient Egyptians kept bees for making honey. Images on tomb walls show that bee-keeping was practiced in Egypt as early as 2600 B.C. The people found that honey was good for healing as well as protecting and strengthening the body.

Egyptians used honey as food, as a flavouring ingredient, in making perfume and for treating wounds

INVENTIONS AND DISCOVERIES

Q **Was mosaic glass founded in ancient Egypt?**

The Egyptians invented the mosaic glass by fusing together pieces of coloured glass. This art form first appeared in Egypt about 1400 B.C.

Glass was invented by the ancient Egyptians over 9,000 years ago

Q **What is the ancient Egyptian system of writing called?**

The ancient Egyptian system of writing is known as hieroglyphics. The hieroglyphic script was developed around 3100 B.C. Instead of alphabets, hieroglyphics consisted of symbols called hieroglyphs, which symbolised different ideas and objects.

Q **What is significant about the toilet seats found in ancient Egypt?**

The first known toilet seat in the world was discovered in the ancient Egyptian city of Akhenaten in 1350 B.C. Ancient Egyptian toilet seats were said to be wooden, stone, or ceramic seats placed over huge bowls of sand!

The secrets of hieroglyphics were revealed to the world in 1799, with the discovery of the Rosetta Stone

Q **Did the ancient Egyptians invent the sailing boat?**

It is believed that the sail was invented in ancient Egypt. Dead people used to be sent to their burials by boat on the Nile. They were accompanied by mourners carrying poles with leather shields. Legend tells that in 3200 B.C., a mourner got tired of holding his pole, so he tied it to the funeral boat he was on. The boat began to sail when the wind blew and the sail was born!

Q **Did the ancient Egyptians invent the potter's wheel?**

The earliest potter's wheel is said to have been developed by the Egyptian people during the Old Kingdom period. The device was a turntable that was turned round and round by hand.

The earliest form of the potter's wheel